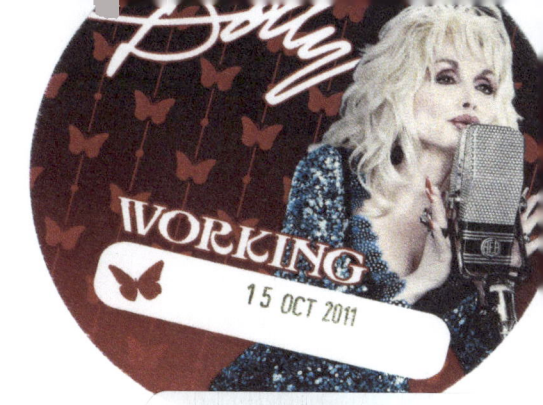

So You Want To Be A
Concert
Photographer

I0470990

Cool Tips, A Few Tricks and Some Insider Advice

By Jeff O'Kelley

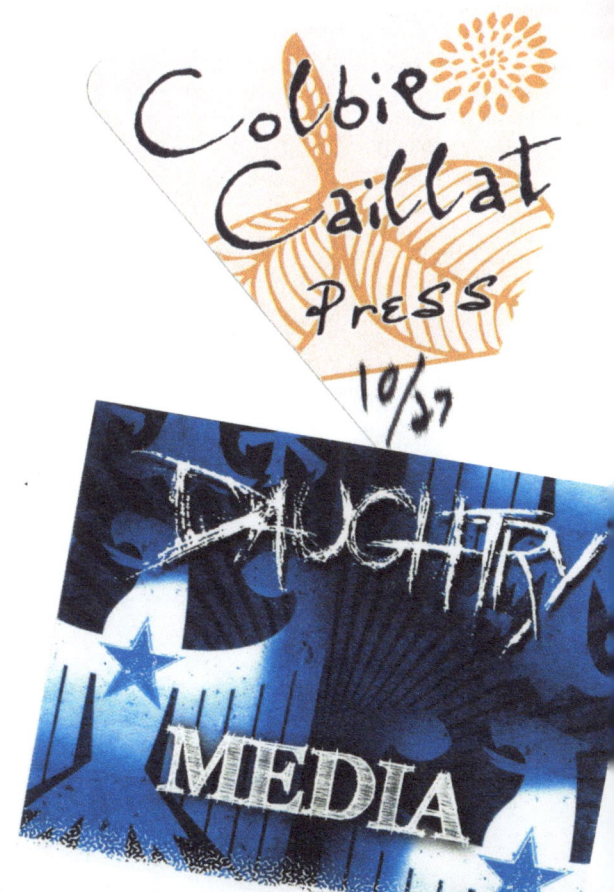

So You Want To Be A Concert Photographer

Written by Jeff O'Kelley

To read more about the author, visit his website at
www.jeffokelleyphotography.com

Copyright © 2012 Jeff O'Kelley

All images by Jeff O'Kelley

First publication: October 2012

Contents

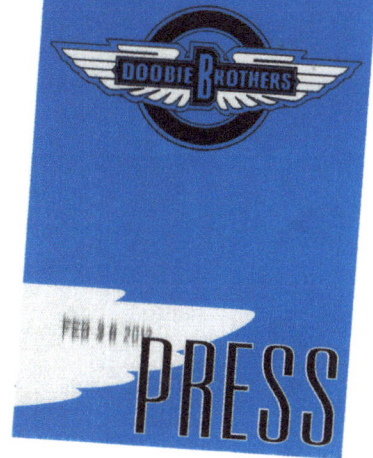

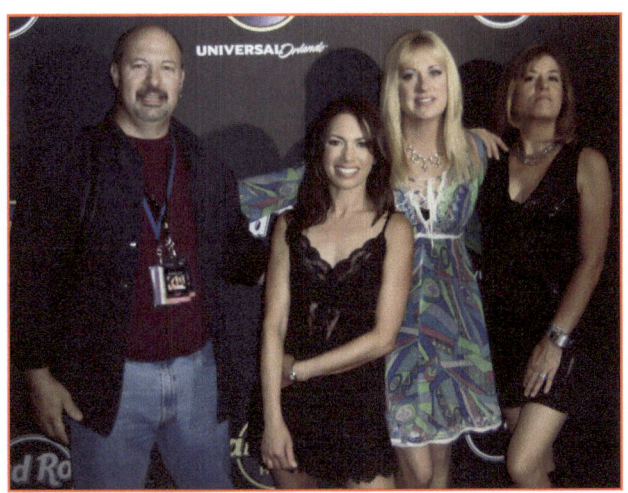

Jeff & The Bangles

Introduction

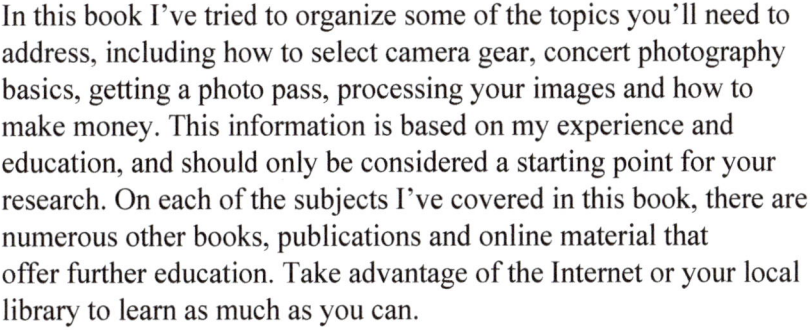

For anyone who is a fan of live music and loves photography, there's no better way to combine two passions. Getting started in concert photography isn't a particularly difficult task, but should begin with some research and planning. Like any other type of business, there are legal, financial and technical issues you'll need to address to avoid running into roadblocks or other problems down the road.

In this book I've tried to organize some of the topics you'll need to address, including how to select camera gear, concert photography basics, getting a photo pass, processing your images and how to make money. This information is based on my experience and education, and should only be considered a starting point for your research. On each of the subjects I've covered in this book, there are numerous other books, publications and online material that offer further education. Take advantage of the Internet or your local library to learn as much as you can.

This is especially true with regard to the legal issues related to concert photography. Take time to research and understand topics such as copyrights, liability and contracts, as they can have a major effect on your business or new hobby.

Now for the fun parts!

Chapter 1
The Right Gear

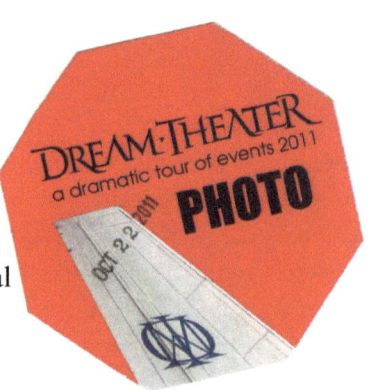

Shooting live concerts is a unique and difficult task. In most cases, you will have no prior knowledge of the stage set up, lighting, choreography or special effects. Given so many unknown factors, you'll need to do a little pre-show homework and be ready for just about anything.

Camera Bodies

I know many photographers who only use a single camera body to shoot concerts. There is nothing wrong with this approach; I even used a single body for many years myself. If possible, bringing a second or even third body to the show will make your life much easier and provide more options, as well as a back-up in the event of a technical failure or accident. There's nothing worse than to get 30 seconds into a show and experience shutter failure, a dead battery or any one of a dozen other possible issues. With only one camera body, you'll be left to watch as other photogs capture all the great shots.

Utilizing more than one camera body will also allow you to bring different lens to the show, opening up your creative options. This is not to say that you can't use different lens with a single body, but I don't recommend it. Concert photo pits are chaotic, dark, crowded and often very cramped places. Not exactly the optimum situation to try juggling several thousand dollars worth of lens and camera bodies.

Your choice of camera manufacturer will also be a personal decision. Nikon and Canon are the most common and, like the division between Ford and Chevrolet truck owners, the debate on which is best is always a hot topic. I use Nikon because that's what I've always used and have a lot of money tied up in Nikon gear. If I ever decided to make the switch, it would be a costly move.

As for the best model for concert photography, I prefer to stay in the middle-of-the-road professional category. For example, I like the Nikon D90 body because it offers the performance, features and quality I need to capture great concert images for less than $1000. Nikon offers several models with more features and options, but the price can easily shoot into the $3000 - $5000 range. Given the near combat conditions that can occur in a concert photo pit, I'm not sure that I want to be worried about the safety of my $5000 camera while trying to grab a few good pictures among the chaos. If you're going to stick to symphony concert photography, go ahead and drop a few grand on a high-end DSLR.

Lenses

As with many other decisions that concern creativity, the choice of lenses for concert photography will vary from photographer to photographer. It's like asking a group of artists which brush is the best; you'll always get a wide range of answers. Ultimately, it will come down to the personal preferences you develop as you become more experienced. It may also be a choice based on cost.

Prime Lenses

50mm, f/1.8 – The 50mm lens is one of the most basic and flexible lenses you can carry. The f/1.8 aperture setting makes it a great low light lens, which can be helpful in dimly lit clubs or concert venues. Depending on manufacturer, you can usually find this lens for less than $200. The only major drawback is the fixed focal length. In some cases, you'll find yourself so close to the action that a 50mm will only allow close-ups of the band members.

35mm, f/1.8 – Same concept and benefits of the 50mm, but the wider focal range offers the opportunity to capture more of the subject in your frame. You can usually find this lens in the $150 - $300 range.

28mm, f/1.8 - The 28mm lens really opens up the stage when you're pressed against the monitors. The price range for this lens shoots up into the $400 $600 area.

Zoom Lenses

Zoom lenses can be indispensable in the pit, as they allow you to catch close-ups and wide stage shots without stopping to change lenses. The focal length best suited for concert shooting will vary, depending on the show set up and from where you are shooting. The biggest issue with zoom lenses is cost, which is typically a function of several features, such as focal range, vibration reduction and aperture. While the vibration reduction feature can add to the price of a zoom lens, the available aperture settings will typically be the leading factor in determining cost.

Zoom lenses are available in two configurations; fixed aperture and what is sometimes referred to as "rolling" aperture. With a fixed aperture lens, such as a 70mm – 200mm f/2.8 lens, you can utilize the full range of aperture settings no matter your focal length. For example, you can choose an f/3.5 setting and it will work at 70mm, 120mm, 145mm or even 200mm. In low light situations, this allows you the full use of your zoom lens without sacrificing the f-stop.

"Rolling" aperture lenses, such as a 28mm – 70mm f/2.8 – 4.0, limit the available aperture settings, depending on the focal length. For example, at a focal length of 28mm, you can choose from the full range of settings. But, when you move up to 50mm or 70mm, your choices may be limited to just f/3.5 or f/4.0. How the lens focal length and aperture combination is calculated is determined by manufacturer and specific model.

So, if the fixed aperture lens offers the best performance, why even consider anything else, you might ask. In a word; cost. While a 28mm – 70mm f/2.8 – 4.0 lens may only run you a few hundred dollars, the price for the same model with a fixed f/2.8 aperture can run $700 or much more. In the end, your choice of lenses may come down to a budget issue.

Types of Zoom Lenses

Wide Zoom – Wide Zoom lenses are typically those that offer a focal range such as 17mm – 40mm, 16mm – 35mm or 28mm – 75mm.

Midrange Zoom – Lenses that offer focal ranges such as 55mm – 200mm, 55mm – 300mm or 70mm – 200mm.

Telephoto – Telephoto lenses typically offer a fixed focal length such as 85mm, 105mm, 300mm or 600mm.

Miscellaneous Gear

Once you have selected the best combination of camera bodies and lenses for you, there are some other items you may want to consider as well.

Camera bag

With all the money you'll have tied up in camera gear, it just makes sense that you'll want to keep it safe. Camera bags and backpacks come in a wide variety of styles and sizes. The choice of which bag to purchase will involve some personal preferences, as well as a few practical ones. Some photogs like the traditional backpack style, while other like the "sling" style that fits over your shoulder like a messenger bag. Try to find one that is comfortable, sturdy, accommodates your gear and, if possible, water-resistant.

Cleaning kit

You can find all types of cleaning kits and supplies for your camera. In most cases, some disposable lens cleaning wipes and a blower brush is about all you'll need.

Flash unit

In most cases, you won't be allowed to use a flash during a show, but it's still a good piece of gear to have in your bag. While most venues and bands stick to the "3 songs, no flash" rule, you will run into situations where it doesn't apply or they just don't enforce it. I've often used a flash in smaller clubs where the lighting is horrendous or non-existent, for outdoor shows where there are lots of shadows on the stage or for shooting artist "meet & greets".

Flashlight

Concert photo pits, backstage areas and venues in general are a dark place once the show starts. To make navigating a maze of road cases, wiring, stagehands and stairs easier in the dark, I keep a small, LED flashlight clipped on my belt loop. Believe me; it's worth its weight in gold if you suddenly realize that you can't see where you're going.

Ear plugs

I am constantly amazed at the number of concert photographers I see shooting without ear protection. Maybe they just don't think ear plugs look cool but, I'd rather be un-cool than deaf. Hearing loss can occur with sustained exposure to noise levels of 90-95 decibels (db), similar to the level of sound produced by an electric hand drill. Permanent hearing loss can result from even short-term exposure to noise levels in excess of 140db, with physical pain starting around 125db. Most rock concerts will typically fall into the 120 – 130db range, but I have personally experienced shows where the music reached 145db in the photo pit.

In my opinion, ear plugs are an important part of my gear. If you decide to wear them, don't go for the cheap, disposable type; look for some good quality ear plugs that offer a significant reduction in sound. I picked up a good pair for about $20, but know fellow photogs that have spent over $100 on high quality, gun range-type ear plugs.

Spare batteries

If you can afford a spare battery for your camera, get one. You never know when one of your regular batteries might decide to die or malfunction. Also, be sure to carry extra batteries for your flash unit.

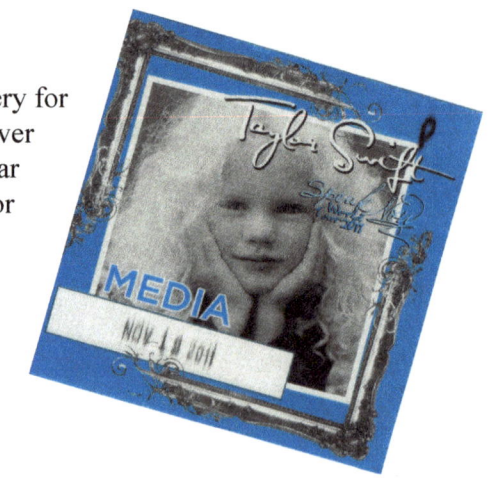

Monopod

A monopod is sort of like a tripod, but it only has one leg. It looks sort of like an adjustable hiking stick with a mount for your camera. While a monopod isn't useful in a photo pit, it can be quite helpful if you are forced to pull out your long zoom and shoot from the back of the house. Even with good vibration reduction lenses, shooting from an extended distance can play havoc with your auto focus and cause blurred images. I've also been known to keep it in my hand for self-defense when forced to navigate dark streets or parking lots after a show.

Plastic bags

There are several manufacturers that sell custom-fitted rain covers for your camera but, in my opinion, they're just a waste of money. Pick up a box of freezer-style, gallon-sized plastic bags and you'll have a good, cheap alternative to expensive covers. Simply cut a hole in the bottom of the bag large enough to accommodate your lens, and then slide your camera into the bag with your lens fitted through the hole. You can operate the camera through the open end of the bag.

One important note; DON'T close the bag. On humid or rainy days, this can cause condensation inside the bag, which is NOT good for your camera.

Shooting in the rain does occasionally happen with festivals or other outdoor events, but you may also need some protection inside the venue. I can't tell you how many times I've had beer, water, soda and other liquids spilled on me during a show. You can also run into issues when the band decides to spray the audience with beer, pull out a bubble machine or, in the case of metal band GWAR, spray the audience and photo pit with fake blood. The best advice I can offer is to be ready for anything.

PRO TIP!
Keep a small, collapsible step-stool in your car in case you have to shoot from the back of a venue, over a concert crowd

What I carry

- Two (2) Nikon D90 camera bodies with added battery grips
- Nikon 24mm – 70mm, f/2.8
- Nikon 18mm – 105mm, f/3.5 – 5.6
- Nikon 55mm – 300mm, f/4.5 – 5-6
- Tamron 70mm – 200mm, f/2.8
- Nikon Speedlight SB-600
- Three (3), Class 10, 300mb/s, 8gb, SD memory cards
- Disposable lens cleaning wipes
- Earplugs
- Monopod
- Gallon-sized freezer bags
- Sharpies

Software

I started photographing concerts in high school, around 1980 or so. Back then, I had to load my own films canisters from bulk film loaders, know the difference between developer, stop-bath and fixer, and be able to calculate aperture and shutter speed in my head, all while manually focusing the lens. Cameras didn't have a nifty LED screen that allowed you to instantly review your pictures to make corrections. You just had to trust that, somewhere among the 48 or so images you shot, there might be a few good ones.

Today's modern cameras are high-powered computers that can calculate a suggested aperture, shutter speed, ISO and automatically focus in the wink of an eye. If switched to the "automatic" mode, most photographers only need to point and shoot.

Even with all this modern technology on your side, not all of your pictures are going to be perfect. Rather than retreating to the dark-room to fix your images, you're going to need the help of some computer software. There are a number of computer software pro-grams that will provide the necessary tools to process your pictures. I use Adobe Photoshop® and Adobe Lightroom®, but you'll need to decide which software you like the best. Most software programs allow you to try out the program for a few weeks and up to a month. This is a great way to check out a program before you sink a lot of money into it.

Chapter 2 – Getting a Photo Pass

Once you've got your gear sorted out and are ready to start shooting, you'll need a way into the show. Unfortunately, there is no definitive, sure-fire way to get photo access to a concert. Getting your hands on a photo pass can take some ingenuity, patience and luck. Every show is different, but you'll soon develop an approach and a list of industry contacts that will make things somewhat easier in the future.

Assignment

One of the best ways to get a photo pass is to be "on assignment" from an established publication. This can be a local daily newspaper, music magazine, entertainment website or bi-weekly alternative publication. Basically, if the band's publicist thinks that the appearance of your photos in said publication will further the band's public image, you'll usually have no problem getting in. On rare occasions, artists will limit photo passes to "major daily papers" or decide that your magazine or website just isn't big enough to earn a pass. Don't get discouraged, it happens to all of us at one time or another. For example, I've never been able to get a photo pass to shoot the band Kings of Leon, despite having an assignment from a major publication. I'm not really sure what the problem might be, maybe I remind the publicist of an ex-spouse or they just don't like my name.

Unless you're on the payroll, getting a photo assignment from an established publication can take some work. Start by contacting publications in your area to ask about their freelance assignment policies. Those who work with freelance photogs will want to see some of your work before they give you an assignment. An online portfolio or website that showcases some of your past work can definitely help your case. Some publications pay; some don't. If you need to build your portfolio or think that a little pro-bono work might lead to future paying gigs, don't be too proud to shoot a show for free. Be cautious that you don't do this too often or you might end up with a cool, non-paying hobby.

Now, I'll stop here to address the scores of fellow concert photogs that balk at the suggestion of shooting for free or complain that those who do it are stealing assignments from working photogs. I'll agree that too many photogs willing to shoot free-of-charge hurts the ability of working photogs to make a living but, just like any other type of business; they have to learn to deal with competition. Besides, many of the same photogs who complain the loudest are the same ones who did the same thing to get started.

I will shoot an occasional show or event for free, if I think that it makes good business sense. If I believe that shooting an artist "meet & greet", special event or venue employee pictures for free might put me in line for future paying gigs, I'll do it every time. In fact, I've gotten some of my most high-paying and steady work from relationships and exposure I've earned from free gigs.

Wire Services

Wire services such as Getty Images®, Corbis Images®, Wire Image® and Splash® hire photographers to shoot events, and then shop the images to print and online publications. Photographers typically get paid a percentage when, or if, the image sells. While getting an assignment from one of the big wire services can help, it doesn't necessarily equal a sure-fire way to get a photo pass. Publicists know that wire services can't guarantee how, when or even if the images will ever be published. Because of this unknown, many publicists and artists won't issue photo passes to wire service photographers.

Web Publications

As print media has started to decline in popularity, online publications and websites are filling the void. Many established magazines and newspapers have focused their attention on the Internet which allows them to publish more content than could ever be imagined with printed publications. This thirst for content often provides opportunities for freelance photogs and photojournalists. An advantage of web publications is the ability to search for work around the world. The biggest disadvantage of working for a web publication is the issue of money. In many cases, music websites are run by a small company or even a single person. They may not have a budget to pay photographers and collecting from a foreign business entity might be tricky.

My best advice is to do a lot of research, know with whom you're dealing and be wary of anything that sounds too good to be true.

Blogs

When blogs first hit the scene, they were mostly considered online diaries or a soapbox for just about any subject. As they have evolved and grown in popularity, blogs have become a more reputable type of online publication and can offer more opportunities for concert photogs.

Since most blogs are run by a single individual, out to make money for themselves, getting paying work from a blog just isn't a sure bet. Consider starting your own blog instead and capitalize on the flexibility and unlimited opportunities that could exist. You can pay to set up a private blog through an Internet hosting service or go the free route with companies such as Wordpress.com or Blogger.com. Getting a new blog established and to the point that publicists consider it a viable media outlet can take some time. You may have to start by shooting local artists or other events that don't require a photo pass. Lots of content is the best way to build a blog, so find a way to shoot as much as possible.

PRO TIP!
www.Examiner.com and www.Wordpress.com are great, free resources for starting your own concert photography blog.

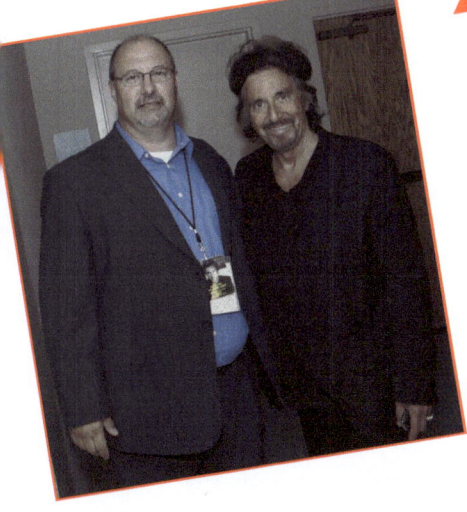

Jeff with Al Pacino

Chapter 3 - On Your Own

If you're shooting on assignment, the publication will typically take care of requesting a photo pass on your behalf. If not, or if you are shooting for yourself, you'll have to put in the request yourself. Sadly, this is not always as easy as it sounds. There is no constant, single point of contact for photo passes. For some shows, the requests may be handled by the venue, while others may require that you contact the band's publicist. Sometimes, they might even tell you who the publicist is, but don't bet on it. It's sort of like the cool, trendy L.A. restaurant that doesn't publish its phone number; unless you already have it, you can't get it. In this case, your responsibilities have now expanded to include a little detective work.

Be aware that timing the submission of your photo pass request will vary with every show. I normally submit most of my requests 2-3 weeks prior to the show. Submit too early and your approval might get lost in the shuffle or forgotten; too close to show date and they may tell you that you've missed a cutoff. In the case of big festivals or events, there may also be a formal application that must be submitted in advance. While I've been able to get last-minute passes in the past, it's typically from publicists or venues with which I have an ongoing relationship. They allow me to slip up once in a while, but it's not always a sure thing.

Once I have a solid contact, I prefer to submit my photo pass request via e-mail. This provides me with concrete, written confirmation of my submission and approval. E-mail requests should be short, professional and include all the information needed to process your request. On the next page is an example of the typical e-mail I send to request a photo pass.

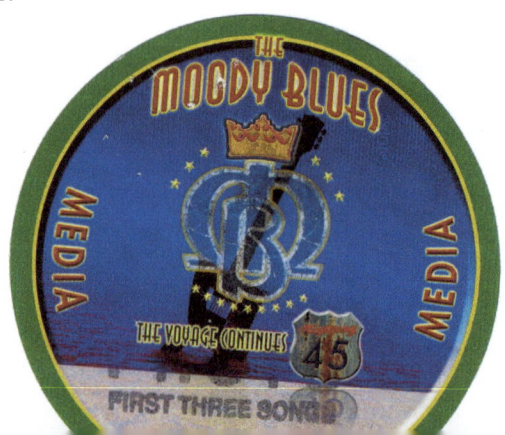

SAMPLE EMAIL

To: publicist@bigbandmusic.com

From: jeff@bigtimephotogs.com

Subject: Media Inquiry: Big Band, Fox Theatre, Atlanta, 9/23/12

To whom it may concern;
I have an assignment from Major Music Magazine to cover the Big Band at the Fox Theatre in Atlanta, Georgia on 9/23/2012. The magazine would like me to supply images to accompany a concert review they plan to publish in the October issue. Can you help with my request for a photo / media pass for this show? If not, can you direct me to the correct person for this request?

Thanks, in advance, for your time.

Jeff O'Kelley
Tel. (000) 000-0000
Portfolio – www.jeffokelleyphotography.com

Never lie or exaggerate when submitting a photo pass request. The publicist may ask for confirmation from the publication or links to your images when they are published. If you get caught lying about an assignment, it could prevent you from getting passes in the future.

No matter how or when you get approval, keep some type of documentation. It's not uncommon to turn up for a show and find out that your name isn't on the list. Having some type of confirmation to show the publicist or tour manager may convince them that you really do have approval. Since 90% of my photo pass approvals come via e-mail, I simply print a copy of the e-mail and take it with me to the show.

Be sure to keep track of any contacts you make, as they may be helpful for other artists or future shows. I keep my contact list in a simple Microsoft Excel® spreadsheet.

The Search

Start your search with the venue. Contact the venue publicist or media liaison to ask if they are handling press photo pass requests for a particular show and how you should submit your request. If not, ask if they can offer contact information for the person you should contact. Some venues are simply "rental venues" which means they are just providing space for the show and may have nothing to do with the actual event. In this case, they may direct you to the show or tour promoter.

If you strike out with the venue, try contacting the band directly. Start with the band's publicist or management. Sometimes this contact information is listed on the band's website or social media such as Facebook or MySpace. In the past I've found lots of good information on the "About" page on Facebook. If this doesn't yield any information, try a simple online search like "Aerosmith publicist" or "Radiohead management". Publicists will often include a list of clients on their website, which will turn up in an online search.

The next place to try would be the band's current record label. Go to the label website and see if they offer any contact information for a label publicist or public relations person. If so, contact them to ask about contact information for the band's publicist or manager. Getting contact information for a record label can be difficult as they try to avoid a barrage of e-mails and phone calls by being hard to contact. Remember the L.A. restaurant phone number; same idea.

When you've tried the direct approach to no avail, get creative. Try contacting the opening or support band about a pass for the show. In many instances, opening acts are eagerly looking for press coverage or just may be easier to reach. Use the same procedure as you did for the main act.

One note on getting a pass from the opening act; in some cases this same pass may not allow you to shoot the headline act. Be sure to clarify that point with the band who gives you the pass or the venue publicist. Even if you can't shoot the headliner, shooting the opening act can offer the opportunity to meet the venue publicist, make some good contacts and provide some great pictures for your portfolio.

No Pass Needed

There are certain situations where you won't need a photo pass to shoot a particular artist or band. For example, concerts presented at street festivals, fairs or amusement parks usually won't require a photo pass. They allow cameras into the event or attraction, and simply can't stop people from taking pictures of the band. You will, however, usually need a photo pass to access the photo pit, if there is one.

PRO TIP!
If you strike out with the band, management or publicist contacts, try reaching out to individual band members. Many artists are easily accessible on Facebook, MySpace or Twitter. Sometimes a direct email request to a band member will get you in the door.

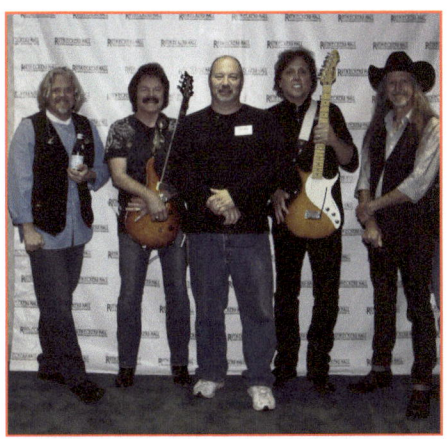

Jeff with The Doobie Brothers

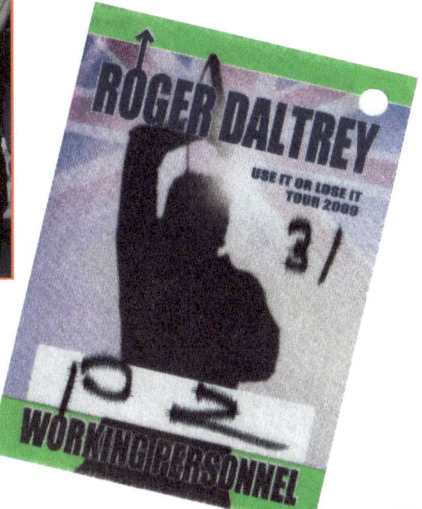

Chapter 4 - The Big Show

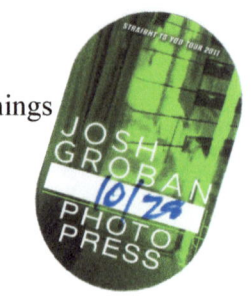

Once approved to shoot a show, there are some things you need to do and know to get ready for the big day. In addition to getting your gear ready, there are some rules and procedural issues you need to know.

Venue Rules

How a venue or event handles press photographers will vary greatly. In some cases, you will meet the media contact at a designated location where you will receive your photo pass and be escorted into the venue. A photo pass is not typically an "All Access" or "Backstage" pass and your access will be limited to certain areas. The media contact may also escort you to the photo pit or other area to shoot the show, and then escort you out of the venue when your time is up. Although I've been to hundred of concerts during my career, I've only seen the first three songs of most.

My experience with most festivals or outdoor shows is exactly the opposite. It's not uncommon to be issued a photo pass and allowed to stay for the entire event, but they may limit access to the photo pit for just the first three songs for each band. Rules for shooting the event usually accompany your photo pass approval.

Gear set up

Shooting concerts can be an extremely difficult task. No matter how much research you've done or how ready you think you are; you still can't be sure what to expect. Don't believe me? Consider this common scenario; you will have approximately 8-9 minutes of shooting time. You don't know what the stage set up will be and you have no idea of the lighting. Once the show starts, your subjects will not stand still, the stage may be filled with obstacles and the lighting will change constantly. You will also have to navigate a photo pit crammed with show security, wiring, cases and other photogs. To make matters even more difficult, the band may employ some really cool effects like strobe lights, fog or confetti just to make things more difficult.

Given the unknown, I start with a common gear set up and adjust as the shoot progresses. Establishing a set up you like will be a personal choice you'll develop after shooting a few shows. Here's my typical set up:

• One camera body with a wide zoom (24mm – 70mm, f/2.8), manual setting, ISO 800, RAW* image format, shutter speed 160, f/3.5, spot metering**, shutter release mode: continuous high speed***

• One camera body with a mid-range zoom (70mm – 200mm, f/2.8), manual setting, ISO 800, RAW image format shutter speed 160, f/2.8, spot metering*, shutter release mode: continuous high speed**

As I shoot the first few frames, I check the images and adjust the settings as needed. Once I'm happy with the result, I don't review any more images unless some element changes drastically.

Some photogs use .JPG format because the smaller file format can speed up frames/sec and they take up less space on your memory card. I prefer RAW format because it offers me complete control over the processing of each image.

** *Spot exposure metering can be helpful since your subject may be brightly lit, but everything around him completely dark.*

*** *Use the speed of your camera to capture as many images as possible. High speed, continuous shutter release can also help you capture some great, split-second shots that you might otherwise miss.*

PRO TIP!
Always format your memory card prior to a new shoot. This can help clear old errors or other issues that might cause problems with your new images.

Planning your shoot

With only a few minutes available to capture as many good images as possible, planning your shoot can help. Everyone approaches a show differently and again, you'll develop a personal preference as you gain experience. I like to divide my shoots into three sections, delineated by songs. During the first song, things can be pretty chaotic and wild, so I like to shoot wide shots to catch as much of the action as I can. During the second song, I switch to close ups and tighter shots. For the final song, I will shoot a mix of each, depending on what's happening. I try to shoot between 250 – 400 images per show. This number of images will typically give you a good mix from which to choose.

Pit Rules

Just like every other workplace, there are rules for shooting concerts from the "pit". Some of these rules are typical, such as the "3 song, no flash" rule, while others may seem to stretch the bounds of sanity. For example, I've been told that I could not shoot the first minute of the show, that I could only shoot the first 30 seconds of each of the first two songs and that I could only shoot the artist from the right side. It may be strange or even comical, but you have to follow the rules no matter how silly or outrageous they seem.

Some common rules and pit etiquette:

• "3 songs, no flash" – The origins of this rule are rumored to have started with The Who's tour manager or possibly even Led Zeppelin. No matter its origin, it's one of those rules that you'll hear at almost every show. Basically, you are allowed to photograph the first three songs of the show and you can't use a flash unit. I have experienced shows where I was allowed to shoot the first 4 or 5 songs, the first 15 minutes or even the entire show. It's entirely up to the artist's management and some are more helpful than others. The biggest rule is: don't break whatever rule they give you. That's the best way to get on the bad side of the venue publicist, tour manager or security. If you want to come back, don't make enemies of the people who get you in.

• Pit versus Sound Board – Every concert and venue is different, so you can't always bet on shooting from the "pit". In some cases, the artist or venue will make you shoot from the front-of-house mixing location (aka the Sound Board), a side aisle or doorway or even the balcony. Even shooting from the pit can be complicated if there's lots of show production gear in the way, special effects rigs, live camera positions, excessive security or an unusual stage shape that limits the size of the pit. I once shot an Aerosmith show where they shoved eight photographers into a 2 ft x 10 ft section of pit area and told us not to move. To make matters worse, the stage was extremely high with monitors and fans positioned along the edge.

• Backpacks –In the concert photography world, we call people who insist on wearing backpacks in the pit "turtles". Given the tight space of a pit, trying to move around someone's backpack, or having it slammed into your arm while you're shooting, is extremely annoying. Make it easier on yourself and your fellow photographers by taking it off during the show. I typically either leave mine in the security area of the venue or tuck it under the stage skirt or behind a speaker during the show.

• Don't touch anything on or around the stage. Artists, crew and venue security may throw you out if you break something, knock over a piece of gear, accidentally unplug something or simply exceed your boundaries.

> **PRO TIP!**
> There may be images or video of previous shows on the Internet to help you prepare for an upcoming concert.

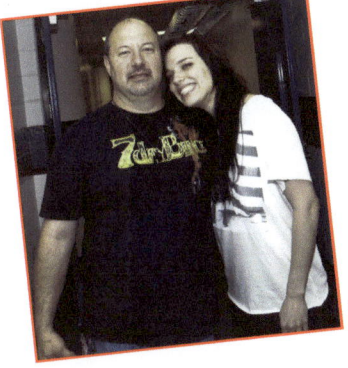

Jeff with Lzzy Hale of Halestorm

Chapter 5 - Image Delivery

Depending on what type of publication you are shooting for and how the images will be used, you may be asked to deliver the images in a certain format.

High Resolution Images

High resolution images may be requested when they will be used in a printed magazine or newspaper, used for posters, on a CD project or other print format. High resolution specifications are usually between 300 – 600dpi and sized to print output size. This means, if the image will appear in a magazine as a 2 inch x 4 inch image, the digital file needs to be sized to that specification. Enlarging an image too much can cause degradation in the image quality. File formats will vary with each publication, but they usually ask for .TIFF, .EPS or .PNG.

Sometimes they ask for .JPG or .JPEG but, since these produce lower quality images, they are not commonly used in the print world. Some publications may even ask for your RAW or Photoshop PSD files so that they can edit them in-house.

"Web Friendly" Images

Images used on the web do not require the same level of quality as print images. Most images are displayed at a size that is a fraction of the original image and in low resolution. This reduces the size of the image file and speeds up loading of the images on a website. Resolution for images used on the Internet is usually between 72 – 100dpi. The size will be determined by the publication or website.

Watermarking

Placing a watermark on your images will help identify your images and prove ownership. It will also reduce online theft or misuse of your images. Software programs, such as Adobe Lightroom®, allow you to create a watermark and apply it to a collection of images during export. Check with the publication that will use your images as to their specific rules on watermarking.

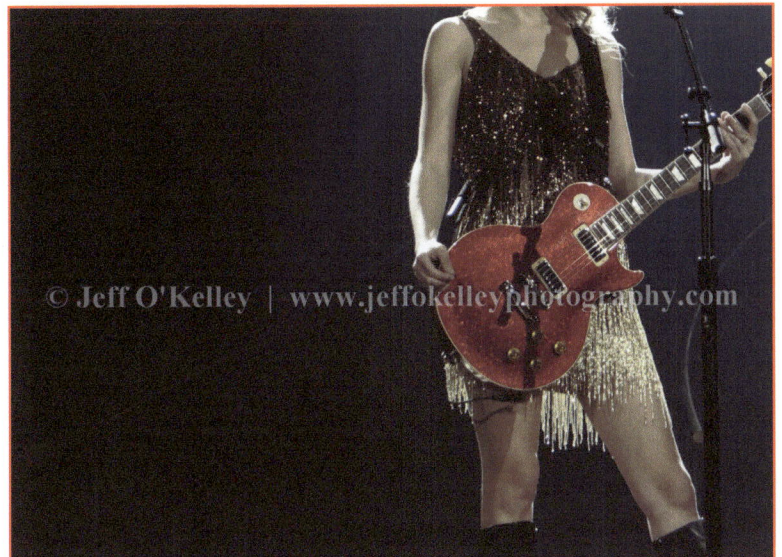

© Jeff O'Kelley | www.jeffokelleyphotography.com

A simple watermark is shown in the image above. This watermark is placed in the center of the document. Publications that allow watermarks will typically ask that it be placed in an area that doesn't obscure the image.

Some publications allow personal watermarks, while others will mark the images with their logo. Many publications and wire services don't allow any watermark, so be sure to check first. Also be sure to inquire as to how the publication intends to protect your images from online theft. Features such as disabling "right click" on images or displaying them in a Flash gallery can help reduce theft.

Another way to protect your images is through the EXIF data contained within the image. EXIF, Exchangeable Image File, contains a long list of image specifications such as when the image was taken, type of camera used, color mode and much more. Again, software such as Adobe Lightroom® allows you to alter the EXIF data prior to export. I suggest completing the copyright section with all of your contact information. This can help identify your image in the future.

PRO TIP!
Make friends with venue security personnel. They can often help with access, tips and can keep your backpack safe while you're shooting the show. .

Chapter 6
Money, Money, Money, Money

Unless you intend to just shoot rock concerts as a hobby, you'll need to learn how to monetize your efforts. Just to be clear, don't expect to make millions as a concert photographer. As a matter of fact, I only know one professional photog who earns a full-time living as a concert photographer. The rest of us have to find ways to generate money from other sources.

Many photogs make all of their income on the front-end, collecting flat fees for assignment shoots. These fees can range from just a few dollars to several hundred, depending on the situation. While it's nice to get money up-front, this is a one-time payment that won't help to build a residual income.

Another option is to work with a publication that offers a combination of up-front and residual payments for your work. For example, I once worked for an alternative weekly magazine that paid about $50 up-front for a few decent concert pictures. The images appeared on the magazine website and I was paid $10/1000 hits. I also received $35 if one of my images appeared in the print version of the magazine. This combination offered a good mix of up-front and residual income for a handful of pictures and a few hours of time.

If you are comfortable with your writing skills, combining your images with a live show review can help expand your market of potential publishers. In most cases, I've found that publishers are looking for a handful of images and a 400-500 word review of the show. Even if you get kicked out after the third song, pulling together a few hundred words is pretty simple. I usually describe the stage set up, comment on a song or two and finish up with some personal thoughts and details on the band's next show. Whenever possible, I try to snag a copy of the band's set list for the show. Including these in a review is a simple way to expand your word count. If you can't get a physical copy of the set list, take a picture of one taped to the stage or road case.

Paying Shoots

There are generally two types of bands; those who can afford promo pictures but won't spend the money and those who really need promo pictures, but have no money. Somewhere in the middle is where you have to find a little income.

For the bigger, more established bands, contact their management or publicist if you get some good shots from a live show. If you've captured some really cool or unique images, they may be interested in some type of licensing deal. While it may be difficult to dig up this type of gig, there is no harm in asking.

Local or new bands may just lack the money needed to get decent shots. This is where you have to consider the long-term viability of investing some time in a new band. Remember, today's unknown band may be tomorrow's superstar. If you feel good about a band, consider giving them some pictures to use for promotion and social media, with the understanding that you still own the copyright to the images. If they decide to use some of your pictures for a CD cover, poster or other merchandise in the future, you can work out a licensing deal for fair use. Even if this doesn't happen, they may decide to hire you as their personal photographer since you helped them in the beginning. For example, I get reoccurring work from a major label county singer that I met when she was just getting her start at the age of 12 years old.

Venues

Many live music venues and clubs employ "house photographers" to cover concerts, special programs and artist "meet & greet" events. These gigs are a great way to expand your portfolio, make some great contacts and pocket some money in the meantime. Since these gigs are prized among freelance photogs, they may be hard to come by, but not impossible. I was offered a house photographer position at a non-profit venue by offering to shoot "meet & greets" for free. Not only did I get some really cool images, I got to meet a lot of artists, tour managers and publicists, while getting in good with the venue. Now, when paying gigs come up, they return the favor. This relationship even got me a gig as personal photographer for legendary actor Al Pacino, while at the venue for an interview/concert. 23

If you can get on with one of the major wire service agencies, such as Getty Images®, Corbis Images®, Wire Image® or Splash News®, your images will be shopped to publications, websites and content providers around the world. When someone uses your image, they pay a licensing fee to the wire service and you get a cut. If the image is used by a major print publication, you could easily make hundreds to thousands of dollars. This is a difficult and competitive market that takes time and a bit of luck. More commonly, I make money from small licensing deals with websites and other online publications which typically fall into the $5-$10 range. I consider this a great way to build residual income and gain exposure.

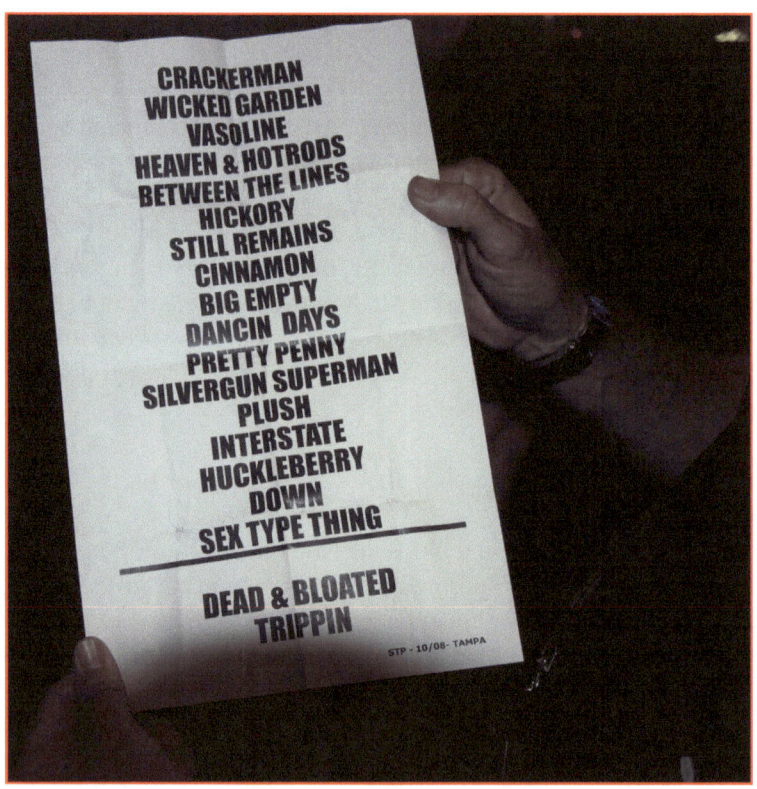

Set list from a Stone Temple Pilots show. I just asked the roadie if I could shoot it before he taped it down.

Chapter 7 – Copyrights, Releases and Contracts, Oh My!

Let me begin this section with a brief disclaimer; I am NOT an attorney, do NOT have any law school education and in fact only know a few attorneys personally. The information I've included in this section should not be considered legal advice or even completely accurate or correct. I am only passing on my personal knowledge and experience as a way to help you get started in the business. Before you embark into the world of concert photography, you may want to spend some time researching legal subjects that apply to you. If you need legal advice, don't take it from me, talk to an attorney.

What is a copyright?

A copyright is a form of protection provided by the laws of the United States to the authors of "original works of authorship," including literary, dramatic, musical, artistic, and certain other intellectual works.

According to the U.S. Copyright Office "Copyright protection subsists from the time the work is created in fixed form. The copyright in the work of authorship immediately becomes the property of the author who created the work. Only the author or those deriving their rights through the author can rightfully claim copyright."

Basically, as soon as an image is captured to your memory card, in most cases you own the copyright. I use the term "in most cases" because, while the copyright law and definition is pretty clear, there are exceptions to the rule. For example, if you are photographing a concert under a "work for hire" agreement with a publication, then the copyright belongs to the publication. Also, if you have signed a photo release or agreement with the artist, their management company or other entity, you may have transferred the copyright to someone else. The issue of copyright ownership is a hotly debated issue in the field of concert photography and will continue to be a topic of discussion in the future.

I would suggest reading about copyright law and how it applies to concert photography on the U.S. Government Copyright website. 25

Photo Releases

A photo release is a legal contract between a photographer and the band that some bands require to obtain a photo pass for a show. Photo releases have gained popularity in recent years and can range from very simple agreements to complex contracts.

In most cases, a photo release will outline a few common points:
• How many songs or a specific time limit you'll be allowed to shoot
• Where in the venue you'll be allowed to shoot
• That the images will only be used for editorial use – You can't reproduce the images and sell them on posters, t-shirts, etc.
• You assume all risk for personal injury or damage to equipment
• You release the band from all liability from claims resulting from use of the images

These types of releases are generally pretty straight-forward, but I have seen a few odd restrictions and rules. For example, on several occasions, the publicist has required me to send images for pre-approval before publication. I've also seen stranger requirements such as not being allowed to display the images in my personal portfolio, but these types of requirements are few and far between.

A "Rights-Grabber" is a bit less friendly version of a photo release. The name comes from language in the release that transfers the copy-right from the photographer to the artist. I don't typically recommend signing this type of release since you forfeit any possibility of future income from your images. Additionally, the artist can utilize your images in any way they want, including posters, CD covers and so forth. This means that they could make money off your work with no obligation to pay you anything. There is also no obligation to give you photo credit. In all, a rights-grabber release is designed to benefit the artist, not the photographer.

No matter what type of release you sign, be sure to get a copy of the signed release and keep it. I usually scan the release and save it with the associated images. That way, if there are ever any questions, you'll have a copy of the release.

One last note on photo releases; if you don't agree with something in the release, ask if it can be taken out or changed. Over the years I've run into numerous situations where the tour manager or other artist contact was willing to strike out a particular line or requirement. For example, one release indicated that I agreed to only display my images on a particular media website for six months. As I explained to the tour manager, I was not in charge of the publication and could not promise that the publication would agree to these terms. She agreed that, since it was out of my control, that particular requirement could be stricken from the release. It never hurts to ask.

Work For Hire Contracts

A "work for hire" agreement is when a photographer is hired to shoot a particular event for a publication or other entity, in exchange for a set payment. The copyright and ownership of the images belongs to the entity who hired the photographer. Although this may sound pretty simple, there are a lot of definitions and examples of what qualifies as a "work for hire" situation. To better understand this type of contract, check out the U.S. Copyright Office website for more information.

As a bit of clarification, a "work for hire" agreement is typically not the same as being "assigned" to shoot a concert by a publication or website. Assignments usually only require that you deliver a specified number of images for publication, but you retain the copyright. Be sure to clarify this point before accepting any assignments.

PRO TIP!
If you don't under-
stand something on a release
or contract, ask an attorney
for advice before signing
anything.

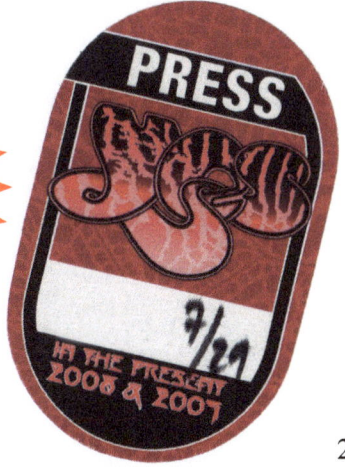

A few exerpts from photo releases I've been forced to deal with recently. The clauses shown on this page display some typical language and restrictions used by many bands today.

Insofar as ████████ and the Entourage are concerned, I shall have the right to use or authorize the use of the Photos solely for (a) publication in the magazine, newspaper, or other periodical set forth below, or (b) television broadcast on the station or in the program, or otherwise, set forth below:

3.   I shall not use, or authorize or permit the use of, the Photos for any commercial or noncommercial purpose whatsoever, other than as set forth above, without your express, prior written consent, which you may withhold in your sole discretion. Further, I shall not use, or authorize, or permit the names and/or likenesses of ████████ and/or the individual Band Members and Dancers in any advertising, promotion, merchandise, or other commercial tie-ups, or in any manner as a direct or indirect endorsement of any product or service.

This confirms that, subject to the terms and conditions of this Photo Release Form ("Release"), ████████ ████████ Inc. ("Company") grants Photographer the right to use the photograph(s) of ████████████████ ██████████████████████and ████████████ collectively professionally known as "████████" (the "Artist"), to be taken by Photographer on the Photo Date solely as part of the article featuring Artist appearing in the Issue of the Publication and only in the Territories. The Photograph(s) shall not appear in any other publication or media or in any other issue of the Publication. This Release expressly precludes any such use.

It is specifically understood and agreed that the name and/or likeness of Artist (or any individual member thereof) shall not be used in connection with the advertising or promotion of the Publication (i.e., institutional advertising as opposed to advertising of the Issue), any merchandising, publishing or commercial tie-ups, or the direct or indirect endorsement of any product or service.

Photographer hereby agrees to indemnify Company, Artist (and each individual member thereof), its management and other agents and representatives (the "Indemnified Parties") against any claims, losses or damages suffered by the Indemnified Parties because of any unauthorized use of the Photograph(s) or any breach by Photographer of this Release.

APPROVED USE: **Press & Review coverage. No other use granted.** *First two (2) songs, left or right front of stage (no center stage!!), NO audience obstruction, NO flash photography.*

Photographer and publication acknowledge that a breach by either or both of the above terms will cause Artist irreparable damage, which cannot be readily remedied in an action at law.

The Photographer and the Publication understand and agree that the Photographer will shoot only from areas designated by ████████████, will shoot only at times designated by ████████████████, will not obstruct any audience view in any way, and will not have access to stage and backstage area. The Photographer assumes all risk for personal injury and damage to equipment and property. The Photographer warrants that Photographer is an authorized representative and agent of the Publication.

Media credentialed to be on site for the "████████████████are permitted to film or shoot stills of songs 2 & 3 ONLY.

TV must shoot from the soundboard with their own cameras, room sound (no line feed) on songs 2 & 3 ONLY. No more than 30 seconds of each song.

The examples shown on this page represent some of the language and demands often found in a "rights grabber" type of photo release or simply restrictions that may infringe on your rights or ability to use the images.

This clause require pre-approval from the band to use the images.

3.   I shall not use, or authorize or permit the use of, the Photos for any commercial or noncommercial purpose whatsoever, other than as set forth above, without your express, prior written consent, which you may withhold in your sole discretion. Further, I shall not use, or authorize, or permit the names and/or likenesses of ███████ and/or the individual Band Members and Dancers in any advertising, promotion, merchandise, or other commercial tie-ups, or in any manner as a direct or indirect endorsement of any product or service.

This clause requires you to give the band your images free-of-charge.

Photographer hereby acknowledges and agrees that the Photographs to be used hereunder are subject to the prior approval of Artist. In addition, in consideration for the rights being granted to Photographer hereunder, Photographer agrees to provide, at no charge, to Company duplicate negatives and/or transparencies (as designated by Company) of the Photograph(s). Company shall have the right to use the Photograph(s) for any and all commercial and non-commercial purposes whatsoever relating to Artist and Artist's activities and Company shall have no obligation to make any payment to Photographer, the Publication or any other third party connected with any such uses.

This clause transfers your image copyrights to the band.

You hereby transfer and assign to us with full title guarantee the entire copyright and all extensions and renewals throughout the world (including by way of present assignment of future rights) and all rights of a similar nature in the Photographs.

This clause denies you the ability to display the images in your portfolio or sell them through an agency

Other than the approved use stated above, photographer and/or publication expressly agree not to re-use or authorize the use of photographs in connection with the above performance to a third party without first obtaining written permission from the Artist's authorized representative. Additionally, no photos / negatives can be placed with any agency or in a portfolio without the written permission of the Artist or his authorized representative(s).

This clause allows the band to sell the copyrights they demanded free-of-charge in a previous clause.

We shall be entitled to assign transfer sub-license mortgage charge or otherwise dispose of our rights hereunder to any person or entity without reference to you.

This clause offers photographers one (1) British Pound Sterling as payment for the rights to my images. Although I circled the section and insisted on my payment, the tour manager declined to pay me.

This letter agreement is intended to protect both ███████ the Artist) and you.

By signing this letter agreement and in consideration of payment by us to you of one pound (£1) (receipt and sufficiency of which you hereby acknowledge) and us and the Artist giving you the opportunity to photograph the Artist on the Date (in accordance with the terms hereof), you hereby agree that

Model Releases

A model release is written permission from the person or people you are photographing, to use their image in a certain way. When you're shooting a band or artist on stage with an approved photo pass, you typically don't need to worry about a model release. In general, editorial use of an image doesn't require a model release.

The requirements change when your images will be used in a commercial way, such as advertising or merchandise for sale. To use a person's image for commercial projects, you'll need a model release. This is especially true when photographing anyone under the age of 18 years.

I have included a very basic model release, which will cover most uses. You can expand on this release by adding details such as the date images where taken, name of concert or photo shot or how the images can be used. Releases that need to address issues such as effective period of release, passing of rights to heirs, assignment or sale of the rights or distortion of the image should be drawn up by an attorney.

SAMPLE MODEL RELEASE

In exchange for consideration received, I hereby give permission to (insert your name or business name) to use my name and photographic likeness in all forms and media for advertising, trade, and any other lawful purposes.

Print Name:_____

Signature:_____Date:_____

If Model is under 18 years of age:
I, (insert name of parent or legal guardian), am the parent/legal guardian of the individual named above, I have read this release and approve of its terms.

Print Name:_____Relationship:_____

Signature: _____Date:_____

Privacy Issues

When in public places, such as concert halls, arenas or other music venues, people have virtually no right to privacy. In general, anyone can be photographed without their consent unless they are in a place where they should have a reasonable expectation of privacy, including locations such as dressing rooms, rest rooms, hospitals, or inside a private residence. This typically applies regardless of the age or sex of the person but, be very careful when photographing minors.

Photographing Minors

While this might seem a strange topic for concert photographers, it may come into play more than you realize. Many of today's bands and artists are under the age of 18 years. Although you are photographing them in a public place with permission, there can still be issues of which you should be aware.

For example, I once photographed a concert by country superstar Taylor Swift, prior to her 18th birthday. As I reviewed my images from the show, I realized that several caught the artist in poses that exposed her in ways that could have been considered lewd or inappropriate. She was completely dressed and probably didn't mean to strike such poses but, these things can happen when shooting 6 frames per second. It was just how she appeared for a fraction of a second and my camera caught it. I decided that the images weren't important enough to risk a charge of child pornography and immediately deleted them. It's just better to be safe than sorry.

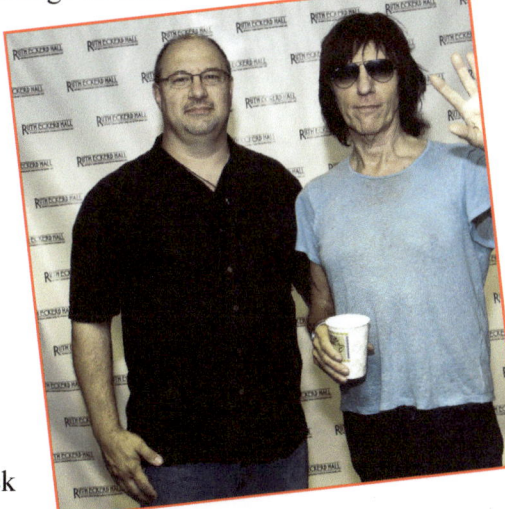

Jeff and rock legend Jeff Beck

That's a Wrap!

At this point, you're probably tired, somewhat confused and a little lost. Don't worry, it's a lot to take in at one time. Concert photography encompasses much more than just snapping a few images and can take some time to master. This book was designed as a simple, quick-start guide to concert photography and only scratches the surfaces of many topics covered. The legal aspects of concert photography alone could keep you busy for months.

Since you don't need to know everything to get started shooting concerts, understanding most of the information I've shared should be enough to get you started. If you're only interested in shooting shows as a hobby, this book will probably be more information than you'll ever need. If you plan to make it a business or career, good luck with your new venture.

You can check out some of my work online at:
www.jeffokelleyphotography.com

If you have questions or feedback, please feel free to e-mail me at:
jeff@jeffokelleyphotography.com

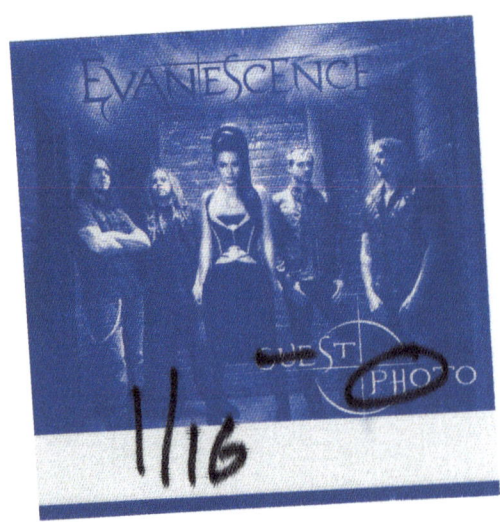

Web Links

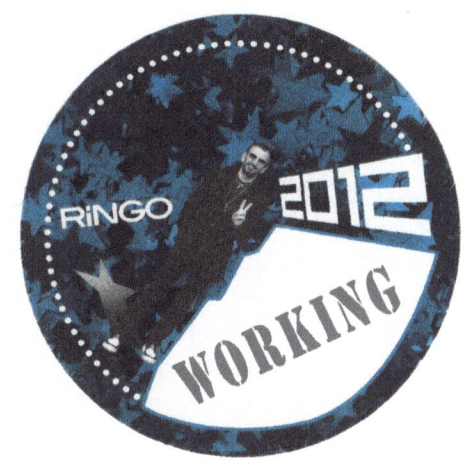

Concert Listings
www.Pollstar.com
www.Ticketmaster.com
www.Tourtracker.com
www.Eventful.com
www.Jambase.com

Manufacturers
Nikon - www.NikonUSA.com
Canon - www.USA.Canon.com
Leica - us.leica-camera.com
Tamron - www.tamron.com
Sigma - www.sigmaphoto.com
LowePro - www.lowepro.com

Online Photo Gallery
www.Flickr.com
www.Photobucket.com
www.Shutterfly.com
www.Smugmug.com
www.Photoshelter.com

Wire Services
www.GettyImages.com
www.CorbisImages.com
www.SplashNews.com
www.WireImages.com

Legal
www.copyright.gov - U.S. Copyright Office

Associations
www.ppa.com - Professional Photographers of America
www.asmp.org - American Society of Media Photographers

Software
www.Adobe.com - Adobe (Lightroom, Photoshop, Creative Suite)
www.Corel.com - PaintShop Pro
www.NikonUSA.com - Capture, View NX

33

About the Author

Jeff is a freelance photographer and journalist, specializing in entertainment topics and subjects. He is currently a house photographer for three major Tampa-area concert venues and has had his images 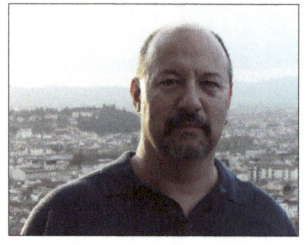 published in a wide variety of online and print publications. His images have also been used by many artists for promotions, websites and social media marketing. Jeff's work as a wire service photographer has landed many of his images in publications around the world.

The Early Days

I got started in photography as a teenager and spent most of my high school years as a yearbook photographer. My "official" yearbook photographer press pass got me into football games, track meets, theater productions and other local events. Since it didn't seem too difficult to gain access to these events, I figured that getting in to shoot a concert couldn't be that difficult. In those days, most concerts were general admission, so getting close to the stage simply meant getting to the venue early. They also didn't have all of the security checkpoints and didn't care about cameras and such.

The first concert I went to as a "concert photographer" was a Kenny Loggins show in Charlotte, North Carolina. I took my Yashica FX-3 35mm camera with a 50mm lens and two rolls of 400-speed, 24 exposure film. It was definitely a learning experience. After waiting a week to get my film back from the drug store, I realized how much more I had to learn. Of the 48 images I shot, I only managed to come away with two really good pictures. They were pretty good and actually won a local photo contest. I was hooked.

Over the years, I have photographed hundreds of concerts that span nearly all genres of music. I have had the opportunity to learn from other talented photographers and hone my own skills in live concert settings. Processing and analyzing thousands of images has allowed me to develop a trademark style and signature to my work, as well as develop many valuable relationships. For me, concert photography is both a hobby and career, and I never get tired of the rush you get standing in the photo pit when the lights go out.